Staying Together

STAYING TOGETHER

40 Ways To Make Your Marriage Work

by
TOM OWEN-TOWLE

Artwork by MILLARD SHEETS

SUNFLOWER INK
Palo Colorado Canyon
Carmel, Calif. 93923

Library of Congress Catalogue Card No. 87-062585
ISBN 0-931104-21-1

For couples everywhere who bravely choose to stay together through all kinds of weather, for better for worse.

MARRIAGE

"It takes years to marry completely two hearts, even of the most loving and well-assorted. A happy marriage is a long falling in love...Men and women are married fractionally, now a small fraction, then a large fraction. Very few are married totally, and then only after some forty or fifty years of gradual approach and experiment.

Such a large and sweet fruit is a complete marriage that it needs a long summer to ripen in, and then a long winter to mellow and season in."

Theodore Parker (1810–1860)

Lest it be thought that this book was written in an idealistic vacuum, I want to assure the reader that the author is thoroughly married to a loving, kicking person who gives and takes in this marriage with equal volume and commensurate fervor. In fact, it is the mutuality of our partnership that inspired Tom to write *Staying Together*.

In our marriage we have experienced a gamut of emotions from ecstasy to sorrow, friendliness to estrangement, delight to disagreement. Yet we endure and forge ahead. By nature we are a fiercely loyal duo.

We recognize that what we are able to achieve together to affect the quality of life around us is more than either of us can do alone. Such an empowering bond can also haunt us when it requires our absolute cooperation during times of upset or discord. Over the years we have resolved to support and love one another through and beyond our differences. It's not always easy, but so rewarding.

I have a vision of wholeness toward which Tom and I are evolving together. I deeply cherish and want the ongoing companionship I have with this man who has influenced my life in unique ways. No other person that I have known has so unswervingly believed in and nudged me into every new territory of growth. We entered together the era of equality between partners. For our entire marriage we have been consciously, often painfully, carving out a relationship in which both of us fully share in the many areas of our lives.

I appreciate Tom for writing this book out of his personal and professional experience. In a time when many couples are endeavoring to build lasting relationships the philosophical/practical support offered in *Staying Together* will prove wonderfully reinforcing.

Carolyn Owen-Towle

"We were made for Joy and Woe;
And when this we rightly know,
Thro' the World we safely go,
Joy and woe are woven fine,
A clothing for the soul divine."

William Blake (1757–1827)

In traditions of Western marriage there are no more familiar words than "for better for worse." This marital admonition from the 1789 Anglican Book of Common Prayer leaves little room for weaseling. No "ifs," "ands," or "buts" are permitted. In the original text there isn't even a comma to break up the two phrases, to give partners an emotional pause. The words are commingled, of equal value, one continuous flow—"for better for worse."

Marriage is not an either/or proposition. Partners don't get to choose either joy or woe. As Blake says, they are "woven fine" and tumble forth unpredictably in our marriages. As the most intimate encounter available to humans, marriage embraces the whole sweep of existence. It invites the bitter, the sweet, and all combinations thereof.

Many of us moderns in pursuit of the pure, perfect partnership labor in vain to rid our marriages of nagging doubts and raging demons. We get married in the first place to be safe and comfortable. We believe the "happily ever after" myth. If we could only eliminate the *worse,* our marriages would end up all the *better*. Or so we fantasize. Alas, life and love don't work that way. Trying to suppress, tame, or transcend life's dark side, rather than acknowledge it, only results in shriveled, puny partnerships.

Along with most of my peers, I was married in my early twenties, barely dry behind the ears. I remember mouthing before God and everyone the words "for better for worse," but I was too immature to know what they would mean.

Now, in my second marriage, I am grown up enough to say, believe, and trust the entire phrase. For Carolyn and I know well both joy and woe, the bitter and the sweet. "For better for worse" matches our marriage.

Furthermore, we are devoted to living that vow forever, because we need all our remaining days to stretch our partnership to its heights and depths. We covet a long, long growing in love. As Auguste Comte said, and we agree, "A whole lifetime is hardly enough to enable two lovers to know each other."

I have come to realize that Carolyn and I aren't alone. Countless other couples I've met, counseled, or married share the same growing commitment.

This book is for and about such partners. It is addressed to couples who valiantly devote themselves to making the most of the marriages they have rather than growing stale, looking around, getting out.

I salute all who face the trials of marriage and survive. Even thrive sometimes.

We aren't extraordinary couples. We aren't always "successful," unless success means staying close and working hard. We don't demand perfection in our selves, our partners, our marriages.

On the other hand, we aren't willing to settle for mediocrity, to ignore problems, to coast, to chase unrealizable dreams. Instead, we try to learn from our blunders, we welcome the wisdom and support of other couples, we pursue counseling when necessary.

We stay married because we know things won't be rosier elsewhere. We stay married because we have more going for our partnership than against it. We stay married because we still believe in marriage, fully aware of its flaws and limits. We stay married because, most of all, we love our mates dearly and deeply, even if imperfectly and clumsily.

The simple, usable suggestions of this book have been drawn from my own marriage-divorce-remarriage experience as well as the breadth of over twenty years of counseling couples in various stages of marital preparation, celebration, crisis, and enrichment.

I call them suggestions because I don't believe any of us can give proper prescriptions for another's marriage. We can only suggest possibilities, offer tips, make invitations, pass on our own learnings. The last thing we marrieds need from outsiders, however well-intentioned or knowledgeable, is quick, easy solutions.

So I offer 40 suggestions to help other committed couples have greater fun and fulfillment while staying married to the same person.

Perhaps you are newly married and need a honest yet hopeful portrayal of how to love, laugh, and last as a couple.

Perhaps you reside in the doldrums of a mid-life marriage and scramble to be more enthusiastic, amorous, and growing alongside your mate.

Perhaps you have been married for decades yet seek renewal for the homestretch.

In any case, if you want to strengthen your marriage, if you wish to woo the one you've already wed, if your vow is to love your partner for better for worse...then, this book may speak to you.

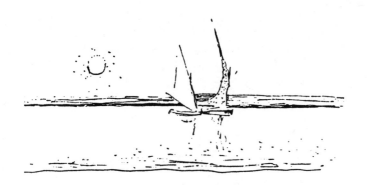

STAYING TOGETHER

I TREAT YOUR MARRIAGE AS THE TOUCHSTONE

Confucius said long ago: As the family goes, so goes the world. He contended that if our homes were in order, so would our communities be, then our states, next our countries, finally the entire globe.

He was right, but I want to go one step further. I believe the backbone of the whole enterprise is marriage. When we partners are at odds, everything surrounding us seems out of sync. When we are at peace with one another, we exude serenity to all whom we touch.

I suggest that we treat our marriages as touchstones, as the primary standards by which we weigh, test, and measure our work, our parenting, our leisure time, our community service.

II LOVE SLOWLY AND STEADILY

*"Love me little by little, be not in haste.
For I would have you love me long. Love
me slowly, love me deeply, love me long."*

Salvador de Madraiaga

You know the excuse used in community fund drives: "Sorry, I have nothing left; I already gave at the office!" That quip describes American marriages.

We give so much of ourselves to our work that our families and partnerships get the dregs. Our homes become the dumping ground for unresolved frustrations or floating irritability we would not dare unload on targets during the day.

Our own marriage often suffers because, after carrying the burdens of our separate worlds upon our shoulders, Carolyn and I have precious little energy or strength to carry one another's. We have been known to love better at the office than we do at home, others better than ourselves, clients more than our marriage.

2

There is an apt poster in a marriage therapist's office which shows a cuddly puppy, head tilted at an angle with a wistful look, that reads: "I don't need a great deal of love, but I do need a steady supply."

That goes for us marrieds, too. We don't desire sporadic mega-doses of tenderness, but daily signs of affection. Myriad and infinite bits of love. Tokens of endearment.

Some examples.

We need to grasp our partner's hand, without a word, before we tackle a tough meeting.

We need our mate to say "thank you" for something we've done a thousand times.

We need to say abrasive things to our beloved in a soft manner.

We need casual walks and serious talks.

We need to respect our partner's opinions even when we find them difficult.

We need full-body love with hands and lips leisurely caressing one another from head to toes.

We need a steady supply of love.

III   CONFESS YOUR FAULTS

*"I'm loyal to a fault. I've got a great many
faults, and I'm loyal to every one of them."*

Steve Allen

I was counseling a married couple
who, after several fruitless sessions,
made a breakthrough when the wife
admitted her reluctance to confess faults.
She said:

> *All our married life, John, I have
> tried to emerge from our tussles
> unscathed, smelling like a rose,
> squeaky clean. I thought I was just a
> sweet gal who wouldn't harm
> anybody. And I wouldn't, except I
> do! I have a self-righteous streak in
> me that won't stop. I now recognize
> that my failure to admit my faults
> does us both harm.*

In an era of no-fault divorce,
husbands and wives need to
acknowledge a full-fault marriage, starting
with their own.

As a married man I have come to
see myself as an alchemist trying to make
precious gold from the base metals of

4

existence. It's tricky, for I am part of the base metal itself.

Let me share with you a funny yet piercing letter that Ted wrote Anna when they were wrestling with their mutual plight of being naggers.

> *Dear Anna,*
>
> *My dissatisfaction with nagging is pronounced because we both are so skilled at it. Like the nuclear powers, neither of us is brave enough to freeze our weaponry.*
>
> *I nag you about the calendar, your work details, and I nag you about your nagging me. You nag me about eating habits, pressuring you, and the like. I nag as a controlling parent; you as a critical one.*
>
> *If you nag me, I am sure to retaliate. I can't seem to back off, go away, or rid my frustrations with some jogging. No, I get sucked in. I don't want to be out-nagged without getting in some of my own juicy ones. We both have to deliver the last, best nag.*
>
> *But, alas, my love, no one wins in our nagging bouts. They are usually draws, and we both end up hurt and upset.*

5

I feel cautiously hopeful that we can grow beyond our picayune underminings. In any case, we have too much going for us to be sabotaged bit by bit by petty naggings.

I remain your buggable and huggable darling.

Ted

Marriages are simply better off when both partners willingly confess imperfections and foibles without always trying to "look good." I don't recommend that any one of us drown in a sea of our own faults. I only invite us to spot, acknowledge and, occasionally, appreciate them. After all, they belong to us.

IV   LAUGH TOGETHER

In a recent survey, several hundred couples with lengthy marriages responded to the question: "What keeps your marriage going?" One of the most frequent replies was, "We laugh a lot together." Not alone, not at one another, but laugh a lot together.

Most of us marrieds could be better clowns alongside one another.

One husband told me, "Individually, Susan and I are funny people. She is the consummate pun artist, and I have a zany, jesting side. But you sure wouldn't know it by our times together. We are so dead serious about improving our marriage that we forget to do the one thing we need most: laugh, laugh, laugh."

This isn't an isolated lament. There is nothing that perks up my own marriage better than tickling Carolyn's funny bone.

Amuse and *amor* appear to be etymological kin. If they aren't, they should be, for laughing will keep us loving. *Amateur* is the term that covers both *amuse* and *amor* and reminds us that in love and marriage we are at our finest when we put our professions aside and relate to one another as rank amateurs, as dabblers, playing uninhibitedly and lightheartedly.

I don't know of one healthy marriage that suffers from too much laughter and playfulness.

V SEEK OUT OTHER COUPLES

Too many marrieds try to make it on their own. Growing couples know better. They seek the support and savvy of veteran partnerships. They participate in programs like Couples Enrichment or Marriage Encounter in order to keep their relationship current, caring, and lively.

One of the smartest things Carolyn and I did as a married couple years ago was to take the Couples Enrichment program that trained us to lead groups ourselves. The fruits have been many.

It has kept our respective feelings and yearnings clear and flexible. It has reminded us to give ourselves weekends away that we wouldn't have taken otherwise. It has shown us that we have more positives than negatives in our marriage. The program affirmed our present partnership, while challenging us to explore new avenues. We took home not only good feelings but also specific tools for enriching our marriage over the long haul.

Most of all, the Couples Enrichment program has given us a cadre of over 100 couples who have shared a similar process and who return regularly to celebrate and strengthen common bonds.

During Couples Enrichment nights, partners are sometimes moved to tears of joy, pain, and laughter. The dialogues over such topics as death, money management, hobbies, and sexual intimacy are enlightening, but simply being close and united with other growing couples is blessing enough. If we did nothing else but eat and sit together in silence, we would feel nourished.

We marrieds all need other brave, committed partners as companions to chide, coax, and console us along life's path.

VI   KEEP SENDING LOVE-NOTES

Lots of couples pen romantic notes during their courtship. Once married, they stop writing.

Yet one of the most loving and sustaining gestures couples can share with each other is love-notes. They can be composed on the run or after personal reflection. Some might be short scribbles, others rambling and philosophical. Some will be outbursts of frustration and confusion, others will be born of unspeakable delight and thanks.

There's nothing quite so touching, or erotic, as finding a note tucked away in your underwear saying "I love you madly" or another one inside your socks with the message "You warm me all over" or yet another nestled in your suitcase while off on a trip by yourself declaring "You are my one and only."

Our marriages hunger for a sufficient dose of both love-conversation and love-correspondence, delivered in fair or foul weather.

VII   BEFRIEND CHANGE

"People change and forget to tell each other."

Lillian Hellman

Marriages that work seem to handle change (both external and internal shifts) well.

First, such couples treat change as inevitable, often desirable. They know that during their marriage each mate will change many times. So will the marriage itself.

Second, unlike the dilemma described by Hellman, solid partnerships stay in close, daily touch—physically, emotionally, and spiritually. Changes, while often anguishing, seldom catch them unprepared.

Third, in healthy marriages, partners focus on changing themselves rather than their mates. As one counselee mentioned, "I am just beginning to realize that you can't make beans grow by pulling on them."

Robert and Alice's marriage made a turnaround when he took responsibility for altering his own habits:

The best way for me to refuel our

marriage is by taking better care of myself. Alice can't exercise for me. She can't feed my mind with the 'right stuff.' She can't structure my time for spiritual growth. All this self-renewal must be initiated and performed by me.

Or as Gretchen recognized during an enrichment seminar:

I've been down on our marriage because I've been down on myself. It's illusory to believe a new husband is what I need, when the real challenge is for me to become a different kind of wife. I can do it. I will change.

Finally, one more suggestion for our marriages with respect to change. The "Serenity Prayer" has steadied many a wobbly marriage. The version that shores up my own marriage during rocky times is:

God,

Grant us the <u>courage</u> to change the things we should change in our marriage, the <u>serenity</u> to leave alone those things we can't fix, and the <u>wisdom</u> to know the difference.

It's a worthy prayer to heed as we travel through many more marriages with our *one* partner.

VIII CLEAR A SPACE FOR EACH OTHER

Someone has noted that most marriages would last longer if partners took regular sabbaths, even leaves of absence, from each other. Why? Because marriages get stuffy, claustrophobic, ingrown.

Thriving marrieds consciously balance times of intimacy with times apart. They take seriously both truths in Gibran's paradox: "Let there be *spaces* in our *togetherness*..."

Here's how it works for one couple. Alex goes to sports events by himself or with a buddy, while Suzanne takes long walks by herself or with a friend. In another marriage Peg works on her stamp collection at the same time that Stan is puttering in the garden. Another married couple claims that one of the keys to their developing marriage is to be able to stay in the same room yet be engaged in different activities. At their best, they can do this for hours. Alone...together.

The 19th century British writer, Matthew Arnold, was a man of many personal interests and community obliga-

15

tions. When asked how he managed to balance his private and public lives and still have time for himself, he replied: "I clear a space."

Expansive marrieds know how to clear spaces for being apart and alone.

IX ENVISION YOUR MARRIAGE AS A COVENANT

"Don't lock me in wedlock, I want marriage, an encounter."

Denise Levertov

A research institute claims that the trend toward increasing economic, social, and sexual options for women has diminished the value of marriage so that women delay getting into it and leave sooner. Marriage just "isn't as good a deal for women as it used to be."

Furthermore, with women balancing jobs, children, and partnership, marriage seems like an overwhelming challenge fit only for superwomen.

Other studies show that men, no matter how often divorced, gravitate back into marriage because of the security and solace found there. In sum, marriage appears to be a good deal for men, a raw deal for women.

Sociological analyses of marriage are useful, but successful marrieds don't feel comfortable at all with "deal" language. Marriage, for them, isn't a trade agreement or a bargained compact. They entered a covenant with their partner; they didn't make a deal, along the lines of the popular TV show.

The difference between a deal and a covenant depicts the difference between a shaky and a sturdy marriage.

In a covenant we make vows toward which we aspire. In a deal you make promises with your fingers crossed.

In a covenant we commit to being energetic on one another's behalf. In a deal you pay foremost attention to *numero uno*.

In a covenant our challenge is to *be* the right person. In a deal you hope to *find* the right person.

In a covenant we realize that forgiveness is the highest form of love. In a deal you are likely to resent or regret incessantly.

In a covenant we endure, come hell or high water. In a deal you last as long as things appear rosy or profitable.

Deals are made and broken daily. A marriage covenant is crafted for the remainder of one's days and nights on earth.

X   BE KIND TO ONE ANOTHER

"Of all the human institutions, marriage is the one which must depend upon slow development, upon patience, upon long reaches of time, upon magnanimous compromise, upon kindly habit."

G. K. Chesterton

There is nothing that strengthens a marriage quite like a "kindly habit." One of the most moving letters I ever read from one of our marriage enrichment workshops was on this very theme. Bruce and Sylvia shared it with our group.

Dearest Sylvia,

You knew I was beleaguered, so you took my place at the council meeting and let me have the evening home alone.

You perceived I needed quiet, so you went downstairs to make your phone call.

You sensed I was vulnerable, so you adroitly sidestepped an explosive topic.

*These and countless other acts of
your kindness are gifts beyond my
deserving, gifts which bring me res-
pite and renewal. I feel loved
through and through.*

*Sylvia, I want you to know that any
act of kindness you show me, no
matter how small, is never wasted.*

*Your behavior has taught me when
in doubt, to be kind, when fright-
ened, to risk kindness, when bitter,
to speak kindly.*

*May our life together be blessed
enough to close in bursts and gestures of kindness, for one another
and those surrounding us.*

All my love,
Bruce

XI KNOW THAT HAPPINESS ISN'T THE GOAL

It has taken me a total of twenty-two years of marriages to realize that happiness isn't the goal. Being mArried is not being mErried.

Here's how I see it, both as a marriage counselor and a partner.

First, happiness is too small and syrupy a state. Joy is the point of marriage, for it includes ample room for pleasure, pain, and all the in-betweens.

Second, you can't bring your partner happiness any more than he or she can deliver it to you. Happiness isn't found or even given. It is invariably created from within or found as a by-product along the journey.

Third, if I say I am happily married, I must also declare "I am sorrowfully married" or "I am frustratedly married" or "I am devotedly married." One could insert any number of adverbs to describe the married condition.

It reminds me of the joke in which, on his 30th wedding anniversary, honest John was heard to say that he had been happily married for at least 15 years.

Half the time is just about right.

XII   SURPRISE YOUR MATE

The most common complaint I hear from modern couples is that their days are so full of commotion and jangle that they appear to be passengers riding different motor boats, barely waving to one another as their vehicles race by.

I offer one New Year's suggestion for all marrieds: spend more time greeting one another, not just when we awaken or go to bed, but serendipitously throughout the course of the day. Surprise one another with lingering embraces, pointless phone calls, and moments of listening to the hallelujahs and hurts of one another's souls.

We couples take our precious, fragile bonds for granted. We check in frequently with our kids. We hail work associates. We call friends. Yet it is the unanticipated greetings from our mates that can make our days soar.

XIII   LOVE BEYOND YOURSELVES

"Love consists not in gazing at one another, but in looking outward in the same direction."

Antoine de St. Exupéry

One of the pitfalls we beloveds face is becoming entranced with one another, inbred, a closed corporation. We must learn to love beyond our own navels or our love means little.

In pre-marital counseling, when couples say they love one another, I reply: "That's fine, but it's not enough. Tell me more. What are the hopes you share in common? Where do you weep, laugh, serve, and rejoice? What is your vision of commitment to the larger world?" After much squirming, they are forced to wrestle with what it means to love beyond themselves.

Yesterday, Carolyn celebrated our wedding anniversary. We spent our share of time gazing at and caressing one another, but we did more. We toasted the fact that our love, at its finest, takes us far, far beyond our nest, our family, our personal bond.

XIV SHARE YOUR STRENGTHS

"As iron sharpens iron, so one person sharpens another."

Proverbs 27: 17

One reason couples endure for better for worse is because they are willing to pit their strengths alongside rather than against each other. They emerge both sharpened and sharper than in their separate existences.

One couple I admire phrased it this way when I queried them about what made their marriage work so effectively.

Bert answered:

It has taken me years to appreciate, but I can now genuinely say that I admire Mary's enormous strength and wouldn't want her to be any other way. Initially, I was both scared by and attracted to her show of power. She was one of the most vigorous, lusty, and strong-willed women I had ever met. Now, at our strongest we whet and hone one another's love.

Mary replied:

Sinewy of body, dogged by a low

pain threshold, Bert's intellectual keenness and emotional verve drew me to him. In his own way he was steely and ironlike, and I felt encouraged to share my power and strength next to his. The truth is that individually neither of us is any great shakes, but together we're an irrepeatable pair, of special mesh, an unfolding mystery, a frequent delight <u>and</u> very strong.

Mary and Bert are "as iron sharpens iron."

XV GIVE ONE ANOTHER PRIME CUTS

The Code of Love, agreed upon by a court of women under the leadership of the Countess of Champagne in May, 1174, said: "Love must always grow greater or it will grow less." Things haven't changed much in eight centuries. If partners don't grow, they pay more for staying the same.

If we don't want our marriages to suffer malnutrition, we must provide adequate nutriments to keep them vital and healthy.

One of the marital myths of our era is the half-truth that love must be natural. If partners always banked on love flowing spontaneously for one another, then we would be victimized by dry spells. Lovers dare not wait around for the spirit or our gonads to stir us. We need to be intentional rather than haphazard in our emotional and physical loving.

Those who put the most wood into the fire get the warmest blaze. So it is with our marriages. When we put major effort and time into our unions, they flame. When we don't, they spit and sputter.

My suggestion is that we give one another prime cuts rather than scraps or leftovers of our time, heart, and passion.

We reap what we sow in our marriages. May the harvest be great.

XVI   SPEAK THE TRUTH IN LOVE

All marrieds would do well to reflect upon a passage from the New Testament: "But speaking the truth in love..." (Ephesians 4: 15) We need to *speak* to one another. While speaking, we are called to risk the *truth*. Yet, always in a spirit of *love*. This simple phrase can keep us on the right marital track.

First, talking to one another sounds like a snap, right? Wrong! The fact is that we couples lead frantic, crammed lives and often don't even connect with one another until our heads are dropping on our pillows.

A recent study discovered that communication adequacy between mates is a direct predictor of marital satisfaction; it was found that, on the average, marrieds in the United States talk to each other only *twenty-seven* minutes a week. That's four measly minutes per day. A marriage counselor friend of mine recommends that couples talk to each other at least two hours a day, if they really want to know each other and grow together.

On a lighter note, you know the story about the Vermont farmer who was the silent type. When he and his wife reached their golden wedding anniversary, he finally broke into a speech that for him was a long one. He said to his wife: "Sarah, I have loved you so much that sometimes I could hardly keep from telling you."

We marrieds need to be disclosing and truthful with one another. We waste time and diminish our marriage when our conversation skirts weightier concerns, fails to be open.

However, there is a distinction between truthfulness and blatant, brutal honesty. Furthermore, there are private parts of our respective beings that will never be visited by our partner. There is a time to reveal and a time to conceal our insides. It is neither possible nor desirable to be open books to one another. As one wise therapist asked: "Would you rather try to be totally honest or have a good marriage?"

That's why the biblical wisdom states: "Speaking the truth in love." Truth has many avenues, but it must always be offered in a spirit of gentleness and compassion, in love.

Speaking isn't the purpose.

Speaking the truth isn't the purpose.

Speaking the truth in love IS the purpose of marriage.

XVII   ENJOY SIMPLE, INEXPEN-
SIVE THINGS

An exercise that I invite couples to do both startles them and enriches their marriages.

I ask them to write down those things they like to do together, then note whether they have actually been doing them.

This process informs partners that most of their shared activities are inexpensive except for occasionally elegant dinners, shopping sprees, and far-flung travels. Most of their marital fun costs $25 or less.

Some of the things my wife and I currently enjoy doing together that are essentially free are: singing, reading, collecting quotes, watching sports, riding bicycles, making love, hiking, playing card games, doing crossword puzzles, strumming guitars, and talking.

You will come up with your own list.

No one can ever put a price-tag on a marriage, but it's sure gratifying to know that most mates truly cherish the simple things in life.

XVIII   SAY "I'M SORRY!"

There is no more important, liberating expression in the marital lexicon than when one partner says: "I'm sorry!" That simple phrase grants both giver and receiver new life, a second chance, healing.

In the book *Love Story* there is the familiar line: "Love means never having to say you're sorry!" I beg to differ. Any marriage worth its salt is full of violation, guilt, apology, and then forgiveness. The words, "Forgive me," "It was my fault," "I'm the one to blame," and "I'm sorry, Dear" are staples in an enduring partnership.

One mate put it this way:

> *When I was growing up, I said 'I'm sorry!' constantly, almost like a broken record, so it became a ritual, immature and vacuous. Now, as an adult, in a committed marriage, I re-own the value of a heartfelt apology.*

XIX DON'T KEEP SCORE

I don't question for one minute the significance of equality in marriage. Carolyn and I have worked hard to achieve it in our partnership, even harder to maintain it.

But I have learned something new over the years. It was brought home by one of our parishioners at her daughter's wedding.

I was accustomed to calling our marriage a 50-50 proposition. Gwen told her daughter and son-in-law during the ceremony to remember that there would be times when their marriage would be egalitarian, but many times when it would be a 90-10, 80-20, 75-25 situation. Her point persuaded me. As partners, we are not always equally involved parentally, sexually, financially, or socially in our marriages.

At any given moment, one of us might be called upon to carry the greater share of the freight.

Marriage isn't always a 50-50 proposition. It's much more complicated than that, and we need to be ready to entertain different moods, flows, and capacities all the days of our marital loving.

Is this not what Genesis 2:18 means when it calls upon man and woman to be "helpmates"? Literally, helpmates are those *mates* who *help* rather than hinder or ignore one another.

Sometimes we find our partner doing more of the helping. Other times, we do more.

The art is not to keep score.

XX   TAKE CALCULATED RISKS

Most of us are mature enough to know that our marriage contains no fast guarantees, only firm intentions and fresh opportunities. We recognize that marriage is a risky business at best, an up-and-down enterprise, from start to finish.

Yet in our moments of panic and insecurity, we marrieds rush to freeze our "ups" and avoid our "downs." When I am tempted to do that, I return to the counsel of a marriage therapist buddy of mine who wisely said:

> *I think of marriage as a ship. A ship in harbor is safe from the elements, but that's not the function of a ship. A marriage is safe, as long as we stay to ourselves or hide our true feelings, but that's not the point of marriage. A partnership comes alive and grows to fulfillment only when mates confront novel challenges and explore new regions.*

Sturdy, courageous marriages know that. They keep sailing together on the stormy seas, taking risks that are calculated but not foolhardy.

XXI   STAY SEXUALLY ALIVE

"There may be some things better than sex and some things may be worse—but there is nothing exactly like it."

W. C. Fields

A sexual relationship is an intensely private matter, ever-changing, and always mysterious. Yet, over the years, I have learned from my own marital experience as well as that of other couples, important sexual principles that keep partnerships alove and alive.

*****

It is the non-genital signs of affection we share that pave the way for our deepest sexual intimacy. The heart remains the most erotic organ in the body with the brain running a close second.

*****

Mutual responsibility needs to be taken for making marital sex gratifying and interesting.

*****

When partners are tired out or bored sexually, I suggest that we consider whether we are masking other concerns.

*****

37

When mates are good and gentle friends, we are better lovers.

*****

Quality in sexuality seldom results from techniques and never from prowess but always from a sense of *equality*. When one's marriage is unequal, lopsided outside the bedroom, we are askew within the sexual domain. Our bodies cannot practice what our minds are not affirming.

*****

Then there are the four F's of sexual love:

First, when we are *faithful* to one another, at all levels, we await fulfilling sex.

Second, when we are *foolish*, playful with one another, our sexual communion is heightened.

Third, when we are *free*, unpressured, mutually consenting, secure enough to say "yes" or "no," our sex soars.

Four, when we are *forgiving* toward each other, affirming the past to be past and granting our marriage new beginnings, our sex life is tender and generous.

38

XXII BE RESPECTFUL

Respect is one of the most underpracticed concepts in marriage.

Gentleness is crucial, so is patience. Love withers without a vigorous sense of humor. But no virtue is more critical to marriage than full-fledged respectfulness.

The litmus test is when we can behold our partner and honestly say:

You and I are equally worthwhile creations. I hold you in the highest regard. Your time, your job, your wants, your dreams are as significant as mine and will be honored as such in our marriage.

We clergy aren't always the finest practitioners of respectfulness. We like to lord it over others, even our so-called loved ones.

The most eloquent commentary I know on this theme was in a cartoon that appeared years back in the *New Yorker*. A minister, complete with collar, is sitting with his wife in his study. She looks fed up, frustrated, furious. He, with an insufferably saintly air of forbearance, is explaining to her: "But, my dear, I AM holier than thou!"

Thank goodness, try as we might, Carolyn and I couldn't get away with such shenanigans in our household, because we are both clergy.

The truth remains. There is no substitute in marriage for respect.

XXIII HONOR *OUR* SIDE

You've heard about the wife who said to the marriage counselor: "That's *my* side of the story. Now, let me tell you *his* side!"

We partners unfortunately carry over some of our competitive habits, for better and for worse, into our marriages. The pursuit of excellence and team-play are laudable drives, but when we conceive our marriage to be a match with two contestants, we've gone too far.

In terms of athletic imagery, marriage is more like a dance, or tossing frisbees playfully to-and-fro, than a hardnosed football scrimmage. Marriage exists for enjoyment not triumph. A victory in marriage is surely a pyrrhic one.

When Pyrrhus, the king of Epirus, led his Greek forces in the third century into Italy, his troops—skilled, equipped, and large in number—defeated the Romans. However, his losses were so substantial that he lamented: "Another victory like this, and I shall be ruined!"

Nonetheless, in the heat of our marital skirmishes, partners get maneuvered into sides: my side and your side. Then each of us tries to emerge victorious.

But I ask us: what does it, what could it mean to win at marriage? Nothing. Nothing at all.

Your side and my side are ultimately irrelevant in the long haul of our marriages. OUR side is all that counts.

XXIV   ACKNOWLEDGE INFIDELITIES

Infidelity, for me, occurs whenever either partner breaks communication or sabotages closeness. Legion are the illicit, passionate attachments that can estrange us marrieds.

She lusts after knowledge and loses herself in books, precisely when he yearns to talk.

He romances sports, as participant and spectator, often as an evasion of personal time with his partner.

The forms of unfaithfulness, you see, are sneaky and varied.

I have found that almost any excessive habit can yank us away from time well spent with our beloved. A friend of ours, whose wife smokes against his will, plaintively moans: "It's as though there were another lover in our room—a lover who pleases her in mysterious ways I cannot."

We marrieds need not pummel ourselves over our peccadillos. That would be too easy. But we must learn to acknowledge that we go awhoring whenever our habits are unduly selfish,

whenever we treat something or
someone as more important than our
marriage, whenever we shun deep-down
involvement with our partner.

XXV   PLAY FOR KEEPS

As a marriage counselor friend of ours aptly remarked: "The couple that *plays* together, usually *stays* together!"

Play comprises a wide, wild range of enjoyment. Play means doing things without a purpose, just for the fun of it. Boy, is that hard for goal-directed persons like yours truly!

Play means spur-of-the-moment trips to the park, late afternoon movies, or mid-day love-making.

Play means Canasta, Gin Rummy, and Rook, all without keeping points.

Play means jaunts to see concerts or baseball games or lazy bike rides around the neighborhood.

What and how we play hardly matters; THAT we play means everything.

Most of us marrieds need to learn how to balance our business *and* monkey-business in alternating rhythm. Too much work makes us dull mates.

I don't know about you, but Carolyn and I resemble the married couple who have read all the psychological and religious self-help volumes on the market on how to adjust to marriage and its challenges. One day they both come to the realization: "Now that we've found real happiness, couldn't we have some fun, too?"

What a pity if we trundle through our marriages regretting that we've overworked and underplayed. It's not worth it.

We are on earth, among other things, to play for play's sake, not to play with a "why" in mind, or with an opponent or with a finish line, simply to play for the sake of playing, because that's who we are—playful, frolicking, fun-loving creatures.

XXVI FIGHT FAIRLY

"Sometimes a scream is better than a thesis."

One marriage was stymied because the couple couldn't muster a fair fight. They always ended up waging a dirty tussle.

In another marriage the husband told me:

> *The hardest gift for me to give my wife is clean, crisp anger. I am willing to debate any day rather than yell. She yells, rages openly, and flushes her system. Her storms pass quickly. I talk, discuss fervently, then, when sufficiently unsettled, proceed to guiltify or harbor a grudge. I've got to learn to fight fairly.*

Here are some guidelines to help our marital scraps be more fair and productive. The particulars are from my own marriage.

First, we avoid pushing one another's buttons, recognize our respective boundaries, and disallow low blows. Past relationships, step-children, and in-laws are typical out-of-bounds areas unless raised by the primary person involved.

Second, we both shy away from money matters, so instead of dumping them all on the other, we divide and conquer the unpleasantries. My wife pays the monthly bills, and I handle the IRS.

Third, I don't criticize her disorderly desktops, and she doesn't parade my fright of car maintenance.

Fourth, I am free to set my own work agenda, but trying to adjust hers is meddling.

Fifth, we both find that our marital abode needs to be brushed, swept, scoured, and mopped, even fumigated, periodically. We tend to leave emotional litter lying around, unattended. We sweep personal dirt and grime out of sight. It only takes one of us to announce that our marriage needs a housecleaning.

By temperament, training, and gutlessness I remain ill-at-ease around marital sparks. Carolyn, being a forthright, occasionally stubborn person, has taught me to stay close and spar rather than pack my gear and scoot.

Let's hear it for the *fair* fight in marriage!

48

XXVII   BE SILENT

"Don't speak unless you can improve upon the silence."

Vermont law

One of the pesky paradoxes of married life is knowing when to talk and when to be silent.

In Thornton Wilder's play, *Our Town*, Dr. and Mrs. Gibbs reflect upon their own marriage as their son prepares for his wedding. Dr. Gibbs admits that his major fear in getting married was that he would quickly run out of things to say to his partner and after two weeks he and his wife would be driven into a quiet, mute state. He dreaded utter silence.

On the contrary, overtalk is the plight of us verbal types. We get caught up in blah, blah, blah—what someone has called "the paralysis of analysis." Silence is usually just the proper Rx for such marriages.

Silence entails more than one or both partners piping down, although that's a good start. There is also silence in the sense of ignoring certain things. "Often the difference between a successful partnership and a mediocre one," wrote Harlan Miller, "consists of leaving about three or four things a day unsaid."

This is a difficult area for many of us. I personally tend to press on when things have gone far enough. My wife, conversely, follows the path of her Grandma Mamie who would prudently announce: "Excuse me, but I need to go into the silence now. Have no fear, I'll return." And she would. And so does Carolyn.

Growing marriages seem to cultivate what George Eliot named "the silent unspeakable memories." They experience silence as a presence.

XXVIII   FIND GROUNDS FOR MARRIAGE

"In every marriage more than a week old, there are grounds for divorce. The trick is to find, and continue to find, grounds for marriage."

Joyce Brothers

In marriage counseling I ask distraught couples to begin with a list of their marital strengths. Starting with positives places a couple in far sturdier emotional shape to deal with their difficulties than if they jump right into their pain.

Stating strengths is strengthening in itself.

Another way marrieds can find, even create, grounds for their marriage is to deliver regular compliments to one another. The size of the compliment is inconsequential. "I appreciate you, Josephine because..." Or "I like you Mel when you..." Or "I admire in you, Jackie, your ability to..."

I married a young couple recently in which I had known the young man since he was a teenager. We had sung and played guitars together around many a campfire.

I was both thrilled and touched when Ernie said to Grace, in a spontaneous footnote to his vows:

"Grace, I can't promise you everything but I will pledge these three things:

> (1) I will stay gentle for that is what attracted you to me.

> (2) I will never fail to tuck you into bed at night.

> (3) I won't give up on us!"

They were already developing solid grounds for their marriage.

XXIX TURN TO THE YELLOW PAGES!

Frequently, we couples try to solve all our problems by ourselves, when we would be better off seeking outside help. This insight came home to me recently when Marjorie and Al told me of their successful solution to a pressing crisis.

Al:
My father, my brother, and I were all clumsy around mechanical things. Still are. I never remember any of us fixing anything that squeaked or leaked. If anyone was adept at repairs at our house, it was my mother. But, more often than not, our family called in outside experts to take care of any structural breakdowns.

Marjorie:
I happened to come from a family of handymen—three brothers and a father. There wasn't anything they couldn't fix. When Al and I got married, I naturally expected him, the male, to overhaul, repair, and fix anything that was broken in our house.

Al:
Marjorie would turn to me and I would turn away, musing "Who me?" I had no experience or interest in fixing things. After all, in our balanced marriage, where we were trying to move beyond sex roles, why in the world was I necessarily ticketed to fix things? Being male had never meant being mechanical to me. Yet here we'd be in a full-blown fight, both interacting with past expectations rather than current realities.

Marjorie:
We finally found a workable solution which we pass on to other married couples in a similar bind. Now, when such a crisis occurs, we ask ourselves: Can Al fix this? Can Marjorie fix this? If either or both of us can fix it, we do it; if not, we turn to the yellow pages!

Al: Eureka!

XXX   DEVELOP A RITE OF RE-ENTRY

Re-entry is undoubtedly one of the turning points in our married lives. Our work situations have inherent delights, agonies, and blahs. Leaving them to go home is a transition that hungers for a proper ritual.

One couple I know has created a workable rite for themselves. I pass it on to you.

Marilyn describes it this way:

After John and I arrive home, we go upstairs and lie down together on our bed, touching yet still. Occasionally we chat, but no shop-talk is allowed, and we do better when we don't utter a word. Being together quietly suffices. This rite of unwinding-and-connection prepares us for parenting, dinner, and evening obligations. Without our re-entry rite, John and I remain frazzled. With it, we are calmed.

XXXI SALUTE YOUR DIFFERENTNESSES

When Thomas Edison was inventing the electric light, he spent years trying to find the right kind of filament, the right gas, the right kind of container. Finally one night, about three o'clock in the morning he made the device glow.

Edison tore out of his lab, into the house, up the stairs and into the bedroom where his wife was sound asleep. "Darling, Darling, look!" he shouted.

Mrs. Edison woke up, rolled over and pleaded: "Will you shut that darn light off and come to bed?"

So it goes in our marriages.

We work our tails off. We produce something worthwhile, maybe even revolutionary, and all we get, from one another, our mate no less, is misunderstanding and rebuke.

The problem is this. We think our vision is earth-shattering but fail to appreciate the dream our partner might be enjoying. If we would be patient, back off, then, when the time is right, we could swap stories.

As close as partners in marriage get, we reside on different wave-lengths. Our worlds can be radically distinct. How could we expect otherwise? After all, every man and woman is an utterly unique creation.

I suggest that we salute our differentnesses of mood, vision, personality.

XXXII   GROW FRIENDSHIPS

Solid marriages are those where the mates are good, dear, often best, friends. When one or the other is thrilled or tormented, we turn to each other. Our partner needs to be one with whom we can reveal haunting fears, grave doubts, and budding dreams.

But that's not enough.

We also need to grow friends outside our marriages. Friends far and wide, ranging from relatives to neighbors to work associates. Friends who come in assorted shapes and sizes, ages and colors, backgrounds and biases. Some will be closer to the husband, others to the wife.

Sturdy marriages learn to modify the Beatles' piece and sing it lustily: "Oh, we get by with a *lot* of help from our friends!"

XXXIII REMEMBER THE MIDDLE CANDLE

"There was this you and this I and this we, which was not exactly you plus me, and which was coming to birth and would surpass us and contain us!"

Anne Philipe

As ministers we are invited to partake of people's most intimate rites. One of these is marriage.

A symbolic ritual Carolyn and I especially value occurs at the candlelighting table. We say: "This lighted candle represents Jill who is a special person. This other candle represents Brian who is a singular human being. Together they light the middle candle to symbolize their marriage, a new reality, a third creation which includes each of them yet transcends them both."

After we speak these words, the couple walks to the table, simultaneously lighting the middle candle with their own candles, and says in unison a variation of the passage from the Song of Solomon: "You are my beloved, and you are my friend."

All three candles remain lighted,

thereby honoring the woman, the man *and* the relationship. One plus one equals three.

Couples are likely to pay sufficient homage to their own candle and are often attentive to the candle of their mate. The weakness lies in our tendency, as partners, to forget about US, feeling that the marriage is doing just fine, when it needs intentional nurture too.

The third candle needs to burn brightly and continuously.

XXXIV FAIL WITHOUT BEING FAILURES

What a freeing notion it is to know that our marriage can fail at this or that, but our couplehood is not in jeopardy.

Sometimes the wife flounders, and the husband is there to pick up the pieces. At other moments he crashes, and she lifts him back upon his feet again. Then there are those inauspicious times when the relationship itself comes to grief, and we need the buttressing of family, friends, or counselors.

The older couples get, the more we realize that marriage is one of the few places in our existence where we can afford to flop and fumble, because there we are truly loved. Countless couples have told me this very thing.

Our special friends Ric and Billie Barbara Masten have been married thirty-five years now, and Ric pays tribute to their partnership with a colorful observation. It is comforting to know, in good and bad times that I can "go home to die with someone who knows just how full of crap I really am."

XXXV PROTECT RED-LETTER DAYS

One of the worthwhile, if not saving, sacraments of numerous marriages has been red-letter dates.

On your respective calendars *pencil* in professional appointments, knowing that many of them will be amended or erased. Then use *black* ink for family engagements. Finally, print the times as a couple in large unmistakable letters with a *red* pen: "OURS."

The red-letter dates are holy, and if broken, the marriage is slighted. Red means stop, pay attention, obey!

Sometimes the red-letter dates are planned in advance; other times they are filled as the spirit moves us. Often marrieds simply stay home and collapse in one another's arms.

Odd-hour movies, "get-away" overnights, meals, walks, quiet times, and much more qualify as bona fide red-letter material.

The red pen underscores the best things we marrieds do with the most important person in our lives.

XXXVI   TAKE THE OFFENSE

"Sex isn't the main lure for extramarital affairs" stated a survey of sex educators, counselors, and therapists. Instead, loneliness, emotional excitement, and proof that you're not getting old are the leading reasons spouses take lovers.

In my counseling experience I have discovered that the best protection against extra-marital enticement is giving *extra* care and oomph to one's own partnership.

The best defense is a good offense.

Successful marriages simply aren't interested in settling for less than they already have. They generate sufficient stimulation and nourishment for one another's needs.

This isn't to say that the strongest of marrieds aren't sometimes lonely, are always "turned on" emotionally to each other, and aren't clearly aging. But they have no good reason to go astray.

They give and receive enough at home.

XXXVII AFFIRM YOUR MARRIAGE AS A POLITICAL EXPERIENCE

John Stuart Mill was on target when he declared marriage to be more than a private bond or even a public witness but ultimately "a primary political experience."

As a minister, I have conducted my share of homemade marriage ceremonies over the years, some extraordinary ones. A colleague of mine had one of his unusual weddings written up in *Time* magazine years back. The vows included:

> *"Gina, do you agree to love Peter more than you love chocolate?" The bride said: "I do."*

> *"Peter, do you agree to love Gina more than the morning newspaper?" "I do."*

I'm all for individual quirks, and I know marriage to be a singularly personal event. Ours certainly is, but the institution remains more than a match of idiosyncratic sentiments and preferences. It is a public event, covering more than the merger of two egos.

In a marriage ceremony we speak our values outloud before a throng of loved ones and witnesses who represent the larger family from which we came, to which we return, whom we need and who need us, from this day forward.

It is public business, this marriage experience. We are not islands, we are peninsulas, connected to the surrounding land. We owe one another love as partners, but we also are beholden to family, friends, foes, and people past and future.

In marriage we submit ourselves to the larger claims of existence, to the survival of the community, to life itself. We enter into a covenant with processes deeper than we know, higher than we can envision. The mystery of what we *do* is more interesting and profound than we two individuals will ever *be*, alone or together.

A married couple's affection for one another motivates and strengthens them to love the world. When we forgive one another, we don't halt there; we are learning how to forgive others outside our partnership.

Some people lose themselves in marriage. Others find themselves in marriage. Neither is enough. The point of joining lives is to gain challenges, worlds,

66

responsibilities, blessings beyond our imagining, beyond our souls, beyond our forts.

It isn't enough to light one another's fire, as glorious as that might be. A vital marriage brings fire, enlightenment, warmth, and blaze to all its surroundings.

May mine. May yours.

XXXVIII   WRITE YOUR OWN LOVE STORY

There are as many love stories in this world as there are marriages.

Yours is neither sensational nor drab. It isn't better or worse than others, simply different. There will never be another marriage quite like yours.

The modern American obsession is to buy marriage maintenance manuals and follow them literally. Readers then turn to their mates and confidently declare: "If our sex life were more normal (which translates into doing precisely what the expert recommends), then our marriage would be set!" Or "If we can eliminate these five marital myths outlined by Dr. Arrived, plus pass the marriage test at the back of the book, then our marriage will be *okay!*"

Phooey! Our marriage will be set only when we begin to pursue the aspirations and face the challenges inherent in our irrepeatable love story.

To be sure, we share much in common with other couples and can learn greatly from professionals, but we are on earth to be originals not second-rate imitations.

A good marriage is like a good casserole. Only those responsible for it really know what goes into it.

XXXIX   MELLOW AND MATURE WITH AGE

At the wedding in Cana of Galilee, Jesus is said to have performed a miracle. The story goes that he converted the water into wine and the steward, surprised, proclaimed that the best wine had been saved until the last.

Growing partners experience both delight and tumult, yet they remain so bold, so hopeful, as to claim that their best years lie ahead of them.

Why?

Because they have been married long enough to clarify their dreams, and are currently blessed with the health and drive to fulfill some of them.

Because they have been married long enough to be familiar with one another's most pernicious habits.

Because they have been married long enough to share what W. S. Gilbert called a "modified rapture," yet yearn for more.

Because they have been married long enough to know that, as with wine, so with love, they will mellow and mature with age.

70

XL PREPARE FOR THE FINAL FAREWELL

"It wasn't supposed to be this way. I was supposed to die first. I had my speech all ready. I was going to look into Gerry's brown eyes and tell her something I should have long ago. I was going to tell her: 'It was a privilege just to have known you.' I never got to say it. But it was too true."

Jim Murray

The agonizing truth is that marriage often ends in sadness. There is divorce or one partner dies first. The final farewell is marked by sorrow.

Years back, at one of our Couples Enrichment renewal nights, Carolyn and I led the session on the topic of "Death and Dying." Some of the questions we discussed are ones all married couples might find useful to address:

(1) What are my personal anxieties and hopes about my own dying?

(2) What concerns me most about my partner's dying?

(3) Do I want to die before my partner? If so, why?

71

(4) What are my wishes for my partner if I die first?

(5) What plans remain for me and my mate to discuss/make concerning our respective deaths?

I'm reminded of the woman who abruptly asked her husband one day, "Arthur, we've never discussed your final wishes. Do you want to be buried or cremated?" He replied, "Surprise me!"

Some of us will choose to be surprised, others not. In either case, the least we can do is coordinate signals with each other while alive.

The Psalmist wrote, ". . . so teach us to number our days that we may apply our hearts unto wisdom." Yes, my days are numbered, so are Carolyn's. I'm glad they are. Knowing our days are numbered motivates us to treat every one as if it might be our last together. And someday it will be.

Therefore, each day we have together is a gift, not to be frittered away but spent resourcefully and lovingly.

Today, July 14, 1987, far from either of our graves, I write:

Carolyn, my dearest, it has been and continues to be a privilege just to know you. And a blessing to love and be loved by you.

EPILOGUE

"A jubilee shall that fiftieth year be unto you..."
Leviticus 25:11a

The average American marriage lasts 9.4 years. Both sets of parents, mine and Carolyn's have utterly demolished the average. They celebrated their 50th wedding anniversaries and show no signs of romantic sluggishness.

Just recently, upon my father's eighty-first birthday, my mother asked him what he wanted and he replied: "You, that's all, you!" As Sam Levenson poignantly wrote, "Love at first sight is easy to understand. It's when two people have been looking at each other for years that it becomes a miracle."

In this Epilogue I want to salute our parents, Mary and Millard, Mary and Harold, four "Dearly Beloveds," for enduring fifty years not of wedded bliss but of married challenge.

There is something powerful, even mystical, in the relational field we call marriage, particularly in the sturdy, beautiful ones. Plenty of wonderful people have sparkled as individuals but failed miserably when married. They have withered in wedlock.

Just think of all the magic involved in fifty years of marriage!

First, in my parents' case, they grew up in opposite parts of America with different religious and ethnic backgrounds. It is startling that their paths even crossed.

Next, among the mingling masses, how did they ever spot one another? Across a crowded room, I suppose. When their attraction blossomed, why was it not like most encounters, one-sided or fleeting?

Finally, to solemnize their private communion and maintain it, through thick and thin, for fifty years no less, is awesome. The sheer durability of it all. You see, I matured in an era when partners made deals such as "Let's stay together as long as we both shall dig it!" or "I'll love you today, tomorrow...and then let's re-negotiate!"

Seriality has prevailed in the marriages of our generation. All six of our parents' children are in their second partnerships. There is no way our current matings will reach the jubilee year unless per chance in nursing homes.

I'm not sure why our parents did so well. I only have hunches.

They must have known they would need long summers and winters to become married. They must have known that marriage was going to be the toughest challenge available—requiring all of the courage, laughter, flexibility, and care they had for as long as it took.

They must have known that they were going to have to hang tough, huddle close, share values, and shape a common vision. They must have learned to be emotionally elastic from start to finish. Plus they must have sensed when to quit talking and what to overlook.

I wonder how they could have learned and sensed all that. They probably didn't at the beginning, but they were tenacious learners and loyal lovers. Apparently, it has been enough.

To love oneself is no easy feat, but to place yourself, in motion, alongside another for fifty years, may just be as magnificent an accomplishment as we humans can manage on earth.

Thanks be to the institution of marriage that has weathered every conceivable human foible and flaw.

Thanks be to these four marrieds and many, many more.

BLESSING

O God,

We invite your spirit to move among all married couples:

> Spirit of unity, remind us, in times of strife and discord, of our common aspiration and shared devotion.
>
> Spirit of joy, fill us with fresh hope when our hearts are heavy-laden.
>
> Spirit of courage, give us the bravery to love deeply, communicate openly, and forgive graciously.
>
> May silence and despair never separate us.
>
> May we ever greet each other, ready for more challenge, comfort, and closeness.
>
> May our lives participate in the ongoing creation. . .giving back love, justice, and beauty to the universe which brought us into being.
>
> May we stay together as growing lovers, for better for worse, today, tomorrow, and tomorrow.

> Shalom and Amen

Mail Order Information:

For additional copies of *Staying Together* send $7.95 per book plus $1.50 for shipping and handling (ADD 6% Sales Tax-CA Res.). Make checks payable to Tom-Owen-Towle, 3303 Second Avenue, San Diego, California 92103. Telephone (619) 295-7067.

☐ GENERATION TO GENERATION, $7.95
☐ STAYING TOGETHER, $7.95

Also available through local bookstores that use R.R. Bowker Company BOOKS IN PRINT catalogue system. Order through publisher SUNFLOWER INK for bookstore discount.